DAY
AVENUE

For Martha Cline,

Sincerest best

wishes,

Frank

Poems by
~~Frank Craddock~~

Frank Craddock
2006

Day Avenue

Frank Craddock

Copyright 2005

ISBN: 1890306916

Library of Congress Control Number:
2005937633

Set in
Bookman Old Style

WARWICK HOUSE PUBLISHERS
720 Court Street
Lynchburg, VA 24504

For
MY FAMILY

And for these names:

Craddock	Anderson
Crowley	Barrett
Rutherford	Felding
Davis	Gibson
Gualtney	Wilson
Waters	Perdue
Driscoll	Smith
Altizer	Dwier
Skelton	Shanley
Windfrey	Gregory
Ketchu	

Special thanks to Ron Robertson, Wiley Francisco and Roy Baugher III

Though I know
it isn't true
it seems
the sun never set
on Day Avenue.

CONTENTS

REMEMBRANCE

As real as a mountain in October
close enough to touch
are the things I remember
clearly, distinctly;

things I do not remember,
memories before my memory,
history, truths I was told
claim and keep as my own;

partial memories
like old photographs
with a head
deep in shadow;

most disquieting
facts which no one alive remembers,
irretrievable pieces of memory,
like lost dream fragments.

I

Grandfather Craddock's Railroad Watch

GRANDFATHER CRADDOCK
d. 22 June 1914

Frank turned back
unlatched the gate
kissed Katie good-bye
a second time;
then with dinner pail and lantern
in hand,
was off.

Climbing Christiansburg Mountain
Little Pepper exploded,
gigantic hunks of boiler
ripped open
like discarded orange peel.

The dead were gathered
in shoe boxes,
no one knowing
what was buried
was all one man.

Frank identified
by the engraved initials
on his railroad watch,
the same initials
left to his
nine-month-old son.

FLU EPIDEMIC
William Pendleton Anderson

My grandfather died
during the flu epidemic of 1918
in Ohio.

He didn't die of the flu
though;
he had gotten over that.

The doctor had been there
the day before
and pronounced him *over it.*

It was his heart, my Mother said.
Papa died of a heart attack;
his heart just gave out.

They had been stopping
with relatives in Ohio
on their way to homestead west.*

Now the dream was dead
and there were three little girls,
the youngest just seven weeks old.

Grandmother sat up
two nights on the train
and brought his body back
(home to Virginia).

---

*No one alive today knows where they intended to home-
stead.

GRANDMOTHER'S GENTLEMAN CALLER

At precisely seven,
every evening
Mr. Paul Seifert,
the epitome of punctuality,
called at Grandmother's door
hat and cane in hand.
At precisely nine
he took his hat and cane
and walked four blocks home.
Both had lost a spouse years before.

They played *Set Back*,
tended canaries
which Grandmother raised.
Twice a week
they walked the five blocks
to the American Theatre
where they watched
The News of the World,
changed bi-weekly,
never saw the movie.

Each Sunday they
attended church and
went to dinner.

There was an occasional
social function:
he was the mayor
of Roanoke.

During Lent,
except for Sundays,

they gave each other up
for forty days.

Mr. Seifert's offer
of an engagement ring
arrived in a very large
cedar chest which he had made
with Grandmother's initials on the front.
The chest arrived
in a large padded bag,
which so frightened my
great-grandmother
that she had Alice call her daughter
at work,
Mrs. Craddock, there's a coffin
been delivered to this house,
and your Mama wants you to come home
right now.
When Grandmother arrived,
she found in the chest
a set of four elaborate, metal boxes
one in the other.*
Inside the smallest was a gift-wrapped box
from Henebry's Jewelers
containing a diamond solitaire.
She wore the ring,
though they never married.

I have only the slightest memory
of a jovial, portly man
who gave me pennies.
He died when I was four.

---

*When Grandmother died, this ring was given to Mother.
When Mother died, the ring was given to Sister Cathy who
is Grandmother's namesake. Tom recently mailed Cathy
the four metal boxes.

When Grandmother died
there were two diamonds on her finger,
my grandfather's
and Mr. Seifert's.

ROANOKE THEATRE
1924

Saturday mornings,
my father about ten,
took his grandmother
to the vaudeville show
where they always sat
on the front row.
Word had it
you couldn't tell
where one towhead stopped
and the other began.

GREAT-GRANDMOTHER

Great-grandmother Crowley,
whom I didn't know,
never understood the radio.

Every time it was turned on
she'd say to my grandmother,
Katie, there's a man in the room.

Grandmother would explain
all over again.
Oh...! Great-grandmother would say,
and that lasted until the next day.

———————

My grandmother, Catherine Crowley Craddock, told
this story about her mother.

7

GRANDMOTHER ANDERSON'S CHOICE

On stout, country legs
she walked the twenty blocks
to the silk mill,
the best job for a young widow
with a one-room-schoolhouse education
and three little girls to rear.

She had the nickel.
One nickel she allotted herself
each day
to buy hot coffee
for the dinner she carried,
or
a bus ride home
after ten hours
standing,
six days a week,
fifty-two weeks a year.

BLACKBERRY HARVEST

Early in the morning of
a late, July day
that Gran'ma had been
counting down
for over a week,
she told the girls
to put on boy's
pants and shirts
because they were going
blackberry picking.
Gran'ma was in her husband's
so they already knew,
but this was the only time
the girls were allowed to wear pants.
All the boys and girls who could walk
were included, except Gran'pa
who had to work in the
blacksmith shop at the Sanitarium;
even the smallest babies were taken
in a handmade, wooden wagon.
Everybody carried as many containers
as possible, and a stick.
The smallest child could carry
two molasses cans as they set off
up Catawba Mountain.
Through the morning heat
laughing and joking
everyone picked
wary of stickers and
watchful for snakes
which hid in the brambles
taking their own Communion.

Bleeding hands and ruby lips
carried the containers home where
enough berries were put aside
for supper, to have an enormous cobbler,
made with rich, sugared biscuit dough,
so large
the big, black pan
filled the oven.
All afternoon
the scent of hot, sweet berries
filled the house
as the rest were
put up against the winter.

Mother told this about her grandmother, Sarah
Alice Cox Anderson.

HOLY HOUR
1952-1956

Sunday evenings
just before seven
Grandmother manhandled
her big easy chair
as close as possible
in front of the TV,
then
settled in
against the gray brocade
to blissfully spend
the holy hour
with Liberace.

FUNNIES

Between church and Sunday dinner
while the big pot was put in the little
when pots and pans flew
and we were only a few
and couldn't read yet,
we sat on the arms of Dad's big chair
in the living room
and he read us the Sunday funnies.
Our favorites were *Blondie,*
Little Orphan Annie,
The Katzenjammer Kids,
but his was
Maggie and Jigs.
When there were more of us,
and the chair arms
wouldn't hold us all,
Dad spread the funnies on the floor.
We gathered,
magpies at a birdbath,
and read the pictures;
leaning out like a giraffe,
he read the words.

DAD'S CHAIR

Occasionally you could
find a penny or two
if you removed the cushion
and with great care
dug way, down deep
in the lining of Dad's chair.

YELLOW ROSE

Mother was a Yellow Dog Democrat,
only made one mistake: Ike.
I could just kick myself.

Lady Bird stopped
at the Roanoke Airport
all in yellow.

Aunt Beulah and Uncle Jake took Mother.
Across the barrier
a dozen yellow roses.

The visit didn't eradicate
the Ike mistake,
but went a long way.

SPARE THE ROD...

A *keen switch* always lived
on the refrigerator
prepared for what might be necessary,
ready to tend to infractions:
little legs danced up and down
on the kitchen linoleum
as the switch flew.
The switch, a bar of Octagon soap
in the top sink drawer,
or a seat on the back steps
usually solved most problems.

If the infraction was major
we were informed
in no uncertain terms,
*Your Father will attend to you
when he gets home;*
which made the rest of the day
sweat.
Then the trip to the
upstairs, back bathroom where
the belt was shown
and a long lecture began,
the worst
of all punishment.

UNCLE BOB*

When he came in
he told her he hadn't
put the horses up,
that he had

just a little plowing left,
he'd finish after dinner.
After they ate
he said he wouldn't be long.

Against the setting sun
Aunt Lula cleaned the kitchen,
snapped some beans for tomorrow
and went to bed.

He wasn't in bed the next morning.
When she went looking for him,
she found him
between the newly-plowed furrows.

All night the horses had stood
harnessed to the plow
waiting for the word
get up.

---

*Great Uncle Robert Anderson

ALICE MACKLIN

Alice's ample arms
were all the security
a three-year-old could know:
Alice and I were buddies.
I was the tow-haired rose
of her eye;
she was my strongest ally.
Oh, Mrs. Craddock, please
don't switch his pretty
little legs,
little legs that could
get into mischief
faster than a rolling ball.

Alice had been
with my grandmother
since my father was a baby.
(Both N&W widows
who had to work.)
Alice was there
with my great-grandmother
as she slid into senility.
Alice, if Mama puts
on her hat and coat
and starts for Mamie's,
drop whatever you're doing
and go with her,
Grandmother said.
Alice went
and made the confusion easier.
(Mamie's could be anywhere.)

When we moved from First Street
to Day Avenue
Grandmother sent Alice with us
five days a week.

Alice lived in colored town
where she raised
prize-winning roses.
When Alice died
(I was five),
Mother and Grandmother sent roses,
went to the funeral,
and
(something I had never seen)
Mother cried.

II

May Procession Sunday, May 1951
Standing, l. to r.: Grandmother Anderson, Michael, Cathy,
Frank, Vincent, Grandmother Craddock
Seated, l. to r.: Loretta, Mary, F. Dallas Craddock, Virginia
A. Craddock, Joe, Virginia, Tom

AT THREE

being slightly dyslexic
I decorated
the newly wall-papered, front hall
as far as I could reach
from first to second floor
with brilliantly crayoned
backward fours,
before there was a remedy.

SISTER

Grandmother Anderson called her
Catherine Ann,
Grandmother Craddock
Catherine,
Mother and Dad
Sister,
we called her
Sis Cath and Cathy.
Regardless of what
she was called,
it never meant
less than love.

VINCE

You stand right there,
and don't you move.
You hear me.
Never questioning
Vince stood *"right there"*
his Easter basket hanging
from his Eton Jacketed arm,
in his short pants,
Buster Browns and high socks.

Cathy found him
an egg
and slipped it in his basket.

A flash from the eyes
of his older brother
gave a lie
to the triumph
over suffering and death
commemorated that day.

You step on the eggs,
so you can't play.
And don't you dare move.

23

MIKE

Michael John
was named for two
great-uncles
who were as much like
fathers to our parents
as possible,
and much like grandfathers
to us,
a proud but heavy patrimony.

Mike was not the middle child
but the middle boy:
probably the longest
on intellect and fortitude
and sticktoitiveness
like a lock-jawed turtle.

MARY
1943

The train Mother took to Washington
to visit relatives
was filled with soldiers who joked,
That woman has a doll baby,
I bet she's retarded.
Sweetie, I can give you a real baby.
An elderly porter intervened,
Missy, you come with me,
I'll find you a seat.
The soldiers had not been
completely off the mark;
Mary was as pretty and placid
as a doll.

EMPERICAL EVIDENCE

At eye level
through the glass bowl
Mary followed the gold fish
eye to eye,
side to side,
fascinated.
The fish will bite,
she was told.
Mary conducted her own experiment
and reported to Mother
fish in hand,
Pish don't bite.
Pish don't bite.

GINNY*

Unaware that her hand had moved
she reached and brushed back a strand of
hair:
fair as corn silk,
soft as bird flight,
gentle as summer wind in sunshine.

WALLACE BEAULEE

Ginny's first boyfriend
wouldn't come any further
than the hedge
at the edge of our front yard.
For hours he stood
and suffered.
He wanted to take her
to the picture show,
but Mother said, *No,
she's too young.*
After several pow-wows
with Grandmother A,
Mother relented
if he would come to the front door,
if Mary and Loretta could go.

Young Mr. Beaulee
was quick to agree.

---

*Mother said she had been born with bangs.

TOM

The shortest distance
between two places
always included a tree.
There was no tree
too tall, too small.
Nothing about life
ever escaped
Tom's wonder and awe.
All trees wore the scars
of his adventures,
and Tom wore the scars
of the trees.

In Grandmother's back yard,
as part of his paper route
going *straight home,*
life demanded payment
for its pain:
it costs money
to drink whiskey
and ride the train.
Neighbors found Tom
broken and unconscious
beside the dead branch
that had given way.
Many anxious hours
were spent in the hospital
those dark, November days.

LORETTA

Retta the youngest sister,
Cathy the eldest;
eight years apart.
They weren't
as much like twins
as Mary and Ginny,
but almost.
They shared a double bed,
every dream,
every fear,
every secret.
When Cathy fell in love
and decided to marry Harry,
at ten,
so did Retta.

JOSEPH

Joe was the baby
and, as with each of us,
the time came
for training.
The small, gray, enameled steed
was brought out
for its final appearance.
The kitchen
the arena for practice.
Soon Joe learned that the linoleum
was an easy surface for travel.
Once when unexpected company called,
not to be left out,
Don Joe rode little Rosinante
into the living room
to Mother's chagrin.

FIRST GRADE

Mother said Sister Angelica
had the patience of Job.
I wrenched that patience
so hard one day
I had to spend recess
sitting in the bottom drawer
of her desk.

EUPHEMISM
for Cathy Smith Bowers

I don't remember
which sister it was
who called down the transom
that she needed a Hershey bar.

Very quickly
a blond head
made a hasty trip
up the back stairs
with a brown paper bag.

Among themselves
the girls were
always full of jokes.
So I passed it off
not recognizing
their Freudian southernism.

AIR RAID DRILL
1942

We were both awakened
by the air-raid sirens.
I have to go to the bathroom,
Sis Cathy called.
I got up and turned on the light.
Immediately
angry footsteps
on the porch,
banging at the door.
In the dining room downstairs,
sequestered behind
closed doors and black-out shades,
our parents playing
regular Thursday night
penny poker.

The explanation
grudgingly accepted:
Just don't let it happen again,
warned the warden.

Friday morning
as usual
the re-rolled pennies
ours to divide.

III

*Grandmother Anderson, Cathy, and Frank
in Richmond, 1945*

ON THE CUFF
Great Aunt Beulah Anderson Dwier

Glistening in the sunlight
from the dining room windows,
Aunt Beulah's depression glass
was marshaled in rows and stacks
behind the frets
of her golden-oak china cabinet:
plundered pink prizes,
impractical dreams for every occasion,
joys on the cuff of sacrifice and want;

delicate bouquets and patterns
embossed, embroidered
like jewel encrusted attire
of exotic design,
devised of necessity
to disguise imperfection:

ensnared at movie theaters,
furniture stores,
at carnivals and fairs,
hidden surprises in packages
at the A&P,
captured at the five and dime;

premiums treasured and swapped
among neighbors and friends
for the perfect match,
a complete assembled set;

standing decades later
silent and ready for inspection,
blushing, translucent beauties,
treasures of a nation's depression.

BATTLEGROUND

As we traversed
the aisles of our classroom
landmined with crinolines and
circle skirts,
to accidentally
penny-loafer a poodle, a tulip
or a dangling chain
might ignite an explosion
that could melt heaven
or freeze hell.

CLOCK

A golden Ivoroid vanity set
spread across the dressing table
in Grandmother's bathroom:
mirrors, combs, brushes,
perfumes, powder boxes,
nail buffer, button hook.
It was the clock
that seized my imagination,
just the right size
to fit a small boy's hand,
an Albemarle Pippin.

What made it tick?
made it run?
was inside?
...tick tock...tick tock...tick tock...

Each visit prompted
further enticement.
Hold it...
mystery...
the secret inside!
The nailfile:
a perfect screwdriver.
The plan complete!

Finally!
lock the door...
explore
the mystery of the clock:
springs, wheels,
cogs turning:
tick tock...tick tock...tick tock...

Never anticipated,
horror struck!
All the parts
would not fit back!

ANDERSON FAMILY REUNION
The third Sunday in July

1

As early as possible, after church,
picnic baskets, hampers gingerly packed,
we set off with aunts, uncles,
cousins, grandparents
for Uncle John and Aunt Edith's
across Catawba Mountain;
hairpin curves coming and going.
Knowing somebody would have a flat
we traveled in tandem
to help repair the inner tube.

The day before
Aunt Edith had cooked the custard,
so Uncle John could start early Sunday
making fresh-peach ice cream,
leaving some churning for us.
We were almost hysterical to get there
to help.
But first speak to all the relatives,
be hugged, kissed;
then churn so hard we often fell over backwards
protesting we still had strength;
older cousins finishing:
we took turns licking the dasher;
ice cream salted down and covered to ripen.

Aunts, great-aunts, mothers,
grandmothers, great-grandmother,
and older, girl cousins,
under the shade of the big trees by the branch,
in a constantly moving circle

doing whatever women kin do,
talking, tending and loving the babies;
all dressed in light, summer cotton
print dresses,
white shoes, except great-grandmother
in black.
To the side, the older men tossing horseshoes
indulgently watched out for younguns:
an occasional clanging and cheer:
a ringer was made.
Noticeably absent during my early years,
the young men, in service,
little and much talked of
circumspectly.

We ran, jumped high and wide
in that golden freedom,
played tag, blind-man's-bluff
hide and seek, snake in the gully,
explored the cabin that had kerosene lamps,
inspected the outhouse at least twice
both inside and out,
wasted water from the pump,
hollered at the Huffman's cows in the side field,
checked the watermelon cooling in the branch,
then went across the old, dirt road
to look at the swimming hole
until dinner was ready, one sharp,
when Uncle John asked the eldest family member
to return thanks
as several aunts fanned the flies away.

Children were served first,
helped by the adults to all we could eat.
The long tables spread
fried chicken, ham, pork tenderloin,

mashed potatoes and gravy, squash with onions,
boiled potatoes and green beans,
cabbage with ham hock,
potato salad, salads made of everything
from the gardens, half a dozen kinds of deviled eggs,
lima beans, fresh butter beans, pork and beans,
plates of perfect, ripe, slicing tomatoes,
cucumbers, pickles of every type and color,
sweet slaw, tart slaw,
pans and pans of biscuits with butter,
apple butter, honey.
Then dessert:
white cakes, chocolate cakes,
pies with, without meringue,
berry cobblers,
banana pudding, rice pudding,
watermelon and fresh-peach ice cream
we had helped make ourselves.
Everything washed down
with crocks of lemonade, ice tea.
Aunt Edith brought out
a 24-cup, blue enamel-pot of hot coffee
made on the wood stove in the cabin.
(Andersons never could get enough coffee.)

(One year Great Aunt Ruth from Bristol
brought a dozen fresh baked, buttermilk pies,
tasted just like lemon.
Boxed: each family could take one home.)

Then time to cover the food
with clean, feed sack tea towels,
rest for thirty, agonizing minutes
before we could change into swim suits,
go to the swimming hole
after cousin Carl's promise

to guard crossing the road and watch us
in water so cold it turned us blue.

Little by little we would wander back,
look under the tea towels for leftovers,
scrap over the last of the ice cream.

Sunburned we were finally collected,
hugged and kissed some more,
packed up to go back to town, falling asleep
after the best day of summer:
Christmas in July.

2

One year my father's uncle,
Mike Waters,
was invited to
the Anderson family reunion.

After dinner
Uncle Mike and Uncle Bernard,
my mother's uncle,
set off up the dirt road
each in his Sunday-go-to-meeting
black suit and tie
and high-top dress boots,
their heads in close animation.

At right angle to them,
running across the road
to the swimming hole,
what could I know
of the reminiscences of two old men
reliving events from their early years
on Catawba Creek.

ADAGE

Like millions
of winged seed pods
that fall from maples in spring,
we were raised amid a rain
of untold adages
which assailed
from every direction.
Grandmother's* advice
to keep from making
a bad situation worse,
The devil you know
is better than
the devil you don't know,
is the one that keeps returning
more often than I would like.

---

*Grandmother Craddock

COUSIN CARL
for Cousin Illamae

Our very own hero,
lifeguard
and football star,
tall and broad
as his mother's easy smile,
a bass laugh that rang the trees.
And he could sleep with bears,
talk with dogs;
snakes were afraid of him.
He was better
than a double feature
Tarzan movie.

IV

Rialto Theatre

THE RIALTO

Each Saturday morning
for three hours
we rode the seats
with the best white-hats
on the range,
rode them hard,
so hard for a double feature
we often had to be
put up wet
absorbing grayless morality
in that first, dark
all-male bonding womb.

Two cartoons and
(as oater insurance)
a serial
of such peril
that we were hung over
until next week.

We called it
The Rat Hole
and viewed with each other
to exaggerate the enormous size
of the nightmare rats *down front*
where only the big boys sat,
rats larger and more vicious
than lions and tigers
sissy girls could catch.

Seven days worth
of shared experience,
day dreams,
déjà vu

(and with the popcorn)
all for 15¢.

BABA

On black, patent leather
high heels with ankle straps
(just like Joan Crawford)
Baba, *no bigger than a minute,*
my mother said,
everyday walked
her little, brown chihuahua
up and down the alley.

With deference due
only to cowboys
we were respectful.

Like Merlin
Baba had magic powers:
she could remove warts,
but not on demand.
A consultation was needed
to see if it was ready,
and it cost a nickel.
Business was good:
there were 50 chaps
in the neighborhood.

With what pride we bragged,
Baba has magic,
Baba can remove warts.
Oh yes she can!
She removed this one right here.
Baba has magic.

The appointment made,
the nickel paid,
Baba would spit on the wart,

49

take a string from her pocket
tie a knot around it
and put the nickel on top.

Soon the wart would go to seed
and fall apart,
because Baba had magic,
she could remove warts.

Baba was Jack Mundy's grandmother. The family
lived around the corner on Franklin Road.

MUD PIES

I remember
the acrid taste
of those mud pies
small, dirty hands made
in the back yard:
patted perfect
moon rounds
laid out
on the hot sidewalk
to bake
and decorated on top
with crushed
red and yellow rock.

BASEBALL

At the bottom of the block,
in the parking lot
across the street,
we played baseball.

We had an old
brakeman's bat
which was either a leg up
or a handicap.

No trouble getting up a team;
we were nine.
Across the alley were the Wilsons;
they were sixteen.

Another couple dozen lived
in our block between Marshall and Day.
Any game you wanted
you could always play.

TEENAGE HUNGER

Three-hundred miles of old, two-lane 460
rose and fell, twisted and wound
through every city and town
and by every courthouse
from Roanoke to Virginia Beach.
With no bypasses then,
a good average was 40 miles an hour.
With luck and no trucks, maybe 42.
The trip took all day.
Six of us fellows left early
passing through Bedford and Lynchburg
to stop at Maude's in Appomattox
for breakfast and an enormous slice
of her famous, home-made apple-pie
high as the sky
with ice cream.
Pamplin City, Farmville, Crewe
Blackstone, Petersburg,
Disputanta, Waverly
all passed on our way to
The Virginia Diner at Wakefield
(in business continuously since 1929).
Blue-plate-special Fried Chicken Dinners,
a small cup of complimentary peanuts,
a hot fudge sundae.
As the afternoon sun grew hotter,
Ivor, Zuni, Windsor, Kings Fork,
Suffolk, Magnolia, Bowers Hill.
Then stopped at a dimly-lit drug store
in downtown South Norfolk
cooled by slow-moving ceiling fans,
and sat on red, covered stools
at the long, black and diamond-chromed counter
for ice-cold, fountain Cokes and Moon Pies.

With the afternoon growing longer,
we finally arrived at the beach
with our clothes stuck to ourselves.
As fast as possible,
changed and headed for the waves.

When the sun began to cool, changed again
and drove out in the country
to Hurds, for a wait in the sandy, front yard,
then sat on the screened porches,
lit with candles stuck in empty wine bottles,
and ordered all-you-can-eat
foot high, seafood platters
washed down with half a dozen pitchers
of freshly made, sweet ice tea.

After roaming Atlantic Avenue
and the boardwalk until late,
we had a hamburger
and a chocolate milk shake.

.

BERNARD

Nardy and I
were best friends;
all we did was fight.
We sat next to each other
everyday at lunch.
His mother made him
peanut butter on Ritz,
mine never did.
We scuffed and scrapped,
rolled in the mud
and tore each other's clothes
because we were best friends;
all we did
was draw lines in the sand,
knock rough edges off
and fight.
Our hike up Sugar Loaf
was a long roll down hill.
Once he kneed me in the crotch;
I thought I would die.
The world kneed him in the head,
now Nardy is dead.
He and I were best friends:
all we did was fight.

A WHOLE NICKEL

A penny, not a problem:
two Mint Juleps.
As fast as my legs could carry me
to Charley Hall's Confectionery,
the penny was gone,
the double symphony begun.

But *a whole nickel*
was a very heavy burden.
Standing eye level
before the glass candy case
filled with more delights
than a camel caravan
could bring from ancient Samarkand,
the sweet misery began,
more often to the disgust
of Charley Hall who could stand
with the little #1 paper bag
just so long
before he closed the case
with a gruff,
I haven't got all day
to wait on you!
When you make up your mind,
you let me know.

Finally the bag was filled:
Mint Juleps, Mary Janes, BB Bats,
Kits, Bit-O-Honey,
Jaw Breakers, a Tootsie Roll.

Occasionally guilt might save
one piece
for Mother.

PASS IT ON

Dinner done, mess kits washed,
we assemble on logs
around the campfire,
the gathering dark at our back,
as our scout leader begins
Pass It On.
Starting slowly
we escape rattlesnakes,
run-away prisoners,
a horse that breaks bad.
As the stars twinkle,
and the velvet forest begins
to moan and sigh,
a mountain lion in mid-air
begins to drop upon
our unsuspecting hero;
an open-mouth pause develops
among the unbelieving ears,
and startled eyes...
Pass it on.
And the storyteller names
the next Homer.

The new narrator
performs an ingenious rescue,
works the story 'round to...
perhaps... a wild boar attack
and then
Pass it on.
Testing our resourcefulness
the story continues
until taps.

That night we sleep secure
in the same knowledge
that saved Ulysses,
Castor and Pollux,
Beowulf, Sir Galahad,
Lash LeRue, and Roy Rogers.

FLUOROSCOPE

In go our shoed feet
at the bottom
of the wooden, art-deco machine
in the children's shoe department.
We peer into eye holes
at the top, click the switch;
our bones appear
through our shoes
phosphorescent gray-blue,
toes wiggling like tadpoles
feeding at the side
of a swimming pool.

Hard to tell
how much damage
we did ourselves
x-raying our feet
every week.

MOUNTAINS

I will lift up mine eyes.

Every kid I knew
figured
everybody had mountains,
held up the sky,
held down the earth.
We were surrounded,
a bowl that had once
formed a lake
not long ago.
(Early settlers found
a tree line,
fossil remains
on the mountainsides.)

What was on the other side?
We climbed them to discover
more.
They sheltered, encompassed,
restricted.

Then we learned
not everybody had mountains.
Our futures lay
in surmounting them.

ELMWOOD

It had been the Tinsley home,
a stuccoed villa on a hill
surrounded by a park,
now the public library:
all the secrets of the universe
at least to a five-year-old.
Take the winding steps
past the empty niche
to the second floor,
the children's section;
sit in the old window seat
and look out on the grass lawn below,
master of all.
Dream the dreams
that are only given
to the very small
before the world becomes old.
Collect six books,
half a dozen voyages and adventures,
and take them home
until next week.

SHELL SHOCK

Waiting patiently
for the Greyhound bus
the back of a white uniformed
sailor boy,
creases starched
sharp as knives.
As he started to board
arms shot up,
he screamed,
no...no...help...I didn't do it...let me go...
please, please...help!
He broke from the line
continuing to scream,
arms flailing
like a windmill,
ran toward the back
of the terminal.
Passing policemen rushed after
as my father hurried me
into a nearby soda fountain
to distract with a coke.

In answer
Dad mumbled,
...shell shocked...

MURDER HOLE!

There was a photograph
in the newspaper:
a black hole bigger than a car.
Murder Hole!
The words reverberated against
the walls of my imagination
as nothing ever had.
A thrill a word;
beyond the ability
of my mind to conjure,
and just over the next county line.

Murder Hole!
Romance greater than
Treasure Island,
Captain Hook,
Blue Beard.
Blood was ice water!

Murder Hole!
I could see it,
somewhere just over
the next county line.

JUNE 6 NOON EDITION

I was not quite six in 1944
when Mother handed me a nickel
and sent me to the corner store
to buy the noon edition of the paper.

Near hysteria was everywhere
on the street, in the store
as I bought the latest news
and hurried to our back door,

There was excitement
and apprehension
that the war was over.
Everyone felt the tension.

The final push was on;
the enemy was on the run,
untold carnage and heartbreak,
the D-Day Invasion had begun.

HOCK

Everybody knew Hock:
a quasi police cap
on his head,
always a clean, white baker's jacket,
shirt and tie,
dark trousers and shoes.
From his neck
suspended on a wide strap
a metal box 12 x 18—3 inches deep
in which there were candy bars
I never knew anyone to buy.
From a strap on his right wrist
a rubber mallet he used
to beat the side of his box
and a whistle he
ceaselessly blew
as daily he traveled
our downtown streets.
Without warning
he would stop,
unintelligibly scream and holler,
fiercely banging the side of the box.
Teenage boys often mocked him
exciting Hock
to throw back his head
and perform more fiercely
his frighteningly frenzied attack.

MERITA BAKERY

Two blocks west,
six blocks north
the square red brick
Merita Bakery.

Certain evenings
with just the right cloud cover,
the wind crossing the hypotenuse,
the air hangs
with home, hearth, safety,
man's most comforting smell.

HEROES

Before revisionist historians,
Richard Nixon
and the sensationalist fourth-estate
we had heroes,
large as the United States,
heroes a boy could emulate:

Davy Crockett,
The Lone Ranger,
President Roosevelt,
Joe DiMaggio.

It felt right to know
a man could achieve the stars,
an ordinary man
could become a hero.

FIVE AND DIME

Saturday always meant
the 10¢ store
toys, candy, popcorn.

Christmas—
a diamond broach
in a padded box
for Mother,
Dad was always delighted
with a 25¢ pipe.

Each counter attended
by a beautiful vestal
not allowed to sit.
No tripod for her
only fallen arches
and sore feet,
iron matron supervisor,
sweat-shop wages,
no union.
Her smile assured
customer satisfaction.

BLUE RIDGE
for John P. Hughes III

Each season has days
when the mountains appear
thin and flat cardboard cut outs,
medium slate-blue
stepping back paler and paler
as they recede
one behind the other
into the horizon
silent as still air.

They hold a truth
only the eye can know
which makes the heart rejoice.

V

MOTHER'S APPLESAUCE FRUITCAKE

Ingredients for a fruitcake:
raisins, nuts, sugar,
spices, candied fruit—
difficult to get during the war years
even with enough ration stamps.
Mother knew:
McClellan's 10¢ Store.
By early fall
the heavy, cast iron roaster
at the bottom of the pantry
began to fill.
The applesauce, bounty,
put up in late summer.

Friday after Thanksgiving,
the turkey carcass simmering
at the back of the stove
steaming the windows
of our small kitchen,
Mother mixed the aromatic ingredients.
Days before we had helped cut
brown paper-bag liners
to fit the bottoms and sides
of the octagonal cake pans,
king's crowns, that had been
our Great-grandmother Crowley's,
tinker mended,
baked caramel brown with use.
The liners greased and fitted into place
the batter was poured.
One cake for each grandmother
the largest for us.
Day long the aroma of fruits and spices
began to tease us toward Christmas.

Weekly apples sliced across the tops
for moisture and flavor.
Not the dense, rich fruitcakes I would come to know,
but perfect for a large family with small children.

Mother bragged,
I never had a sick child
at Christmas.

As each of us left home a cake followed,
apron strings connecting.
The first across the Pacific to Japan,
one to Turkey and Germany.
Cakes crossed Maryland, New Jersey,
New York, Connecticut on their way to Boston;
across the Mississippi to Tucson and Phoenix.
Closer home, over the Blue Ridge Mountains,
to Charlottesville, Richmond;
south by Belmont Abbey (Dad's school),
over the Yadkin River
through Cowpens to Spartanburg,
and one on to Georgia.
Mother baked them,
Dad wrapped and mailed them.

I have wonderful Christmas memories:
the hush of Midnight Mass,
a real bird's nest for the tree,
carols sung-along
with Kate Smith on the radio,
little Christopher playing Santa Claus,
family and friends for holiday dinners;
but no memory is as strong
or lasted as long
as
Mother's Applesauce Fruitcake.

SNOW ICE CREAM

How we wished away our little lives
waiting for that second snow.
(The first
pronounced too dirty.)

Then kneel in the clean white,
brush away the top
and fill a dishpan
to heaping.

Oh, so carefully
fold in the cream, the sugar,
the aromatic vanilla.
(Can you smell it?)

The reward of impatience:
snow ice cream
like childhood
fleeting, sweet.

OH! CHRISTMAS TREE!

A tree is to climb
every boy of three or four
learns in time,
but when it came
crashing down
destroying far more
than four and twenty
glass ornaments
that smashed the floor
like cannons
exploding in war,
I was more astounded
than the fallen angel
that never before
had put a foot
to the floor.

SANTA HOP

I was hopping long before
we left home.
Hop...hop...
Stopped at Grandmother's.
Dallas, I think that boy needs to go
to the bathroom.
Son, do you need to go?
No, Sir.
Let's try anyway.
No blood from a turnip.
Hop...hop...

Cathy wasn't hopping.
She saw Santa first
but couldn't talk.
Daddy had to answer,
Sister wants a doll baby

Well, little girl, we'll see
what we can do.
Merry Christmas!

Daddy whispered in my ear,
Remember, only two things.

Have you been a good
little boy?
Yes, Santa! I declared.
And what do you want for Christmas?

I want a tricycle
and a Roy Rogers gun and holster
and a drumandapaintset.

Well, we'll see what we can do.
Ho,ho,ho!

As I hopped from Santa's lap,
one of his knees was
redder than the other.

FINDING SANTA

What the first worm
of doubt was
I'm not sure.
Your mother and daddy really are...
There isn't any...
Did Santa Claus himself
up close
begin to come unglued?
Something in the newspaper,
a cartoon in a magazine,
a joke on the radio?
Were there too many Santas?

So the hunt began
like wading under water:
a fear of confirming what
I did not want to know.

But there it was
in the back hall
under the steps
in the dark,
the Holy Grail of Christmas.
A first loss of innocence,
too soon.

With both jaw and stomach
on the floor,
several visits were needed
to confirm it wasn't a mirage.

Finally the tearful confrontation.
But as one door closed
another opened,

Yes, son, it's true
but you mustn't tell the others.
Let it be our secret;
they'll find out soon enough.

*Grandmother Craddock dressed in her
wedding clothes, ca. 1911
Suit was made by S. H. Heironimus,
Roanoke, Virginia*

GODCHILD
Aug. 2, 1969-Nov. 10, 1970

On the right side
of the family headstone
in an infant plot
she lies beneath the grass
with her grandparents
and great-grandparents.

Cancer before two.

There are flowers on her grave today;
she would be thirty-five.
By proxy I was her godfather,
but I never saw little Sarah,
nor held her in my arms.

The child of Mary Craddock Rutherford and Jim
Rutherford.

4

UNITED STATES OF AMERICA
OFFICE OF PRICE ADMINISTRATION

WAR RATION BOOK FOUR

Issued to _Virginia R Craddock_
(Print first, middle, and last names)

Complete address _335 Day Ave SW_
Roanoke Va

READ BEFORE SIGNING

In accepting this book, I recognize that it remains the property of the United States Government. I will use it only in the manner and for the purposes authorized by the Office of Price Administration.

_____
(Signature)

Void if Altered

It is a criminal offense to violate rationing regulations.   16—35570-1

OPA Form R-145

THE CHESAPEAKE AND POTOMAC TELEPHONE CO.
OF VIRGINIA

WHEN PAYING IN PERSON, PLEASE PRESENT THIS BILL AND STUB

AUGUST 19, 1945

2-6559   MR. F. D. CRADDOCK JR
RKE   335 DAY AV SW-16

BALANCE DUE ON ACCOUNT (IF PAID, PLEASE DEDUCT FROM TOTAL)

LOCAL SERVICE AUG. 19 THROUGH SEPT. 18

TOLL SERVICE AND TELEGRAMS (STATEMENT ENCLOSED SHOWING CHARGES AND U. S. TAX)....(INCL. U. S. TAX OF   .45)   3.45

DIRECTORY ADVERTISING AUG. 19 THROUGH SEPT. 18   23

Thank You

PAYABLE ON OR BEFORE SEPTEMBER 8   TOTAL   3 68 *